ISBN: 1-57051-030-X

Cover/interior:
Koechel Peterson & Associates

Printed in Singapore

Grandmothers Are for Loving

Brownlow

Brownlow Publishing Company, Inc.

Little Treasures
Miniature Books

A Little Cup of Tea

All Things Great & Small

Angels of Friendship

Baby's First Little Bible

Cherished Bible Stories

Dear Teacher

Faith

For My Secret Pal

*From Friend
to Friend*

*Grandmothers are
for Loving*

Hope

Love

Mother

My Sister, My Friend

Precious Are the Promises

Quilted Hearts

Soft as the Voice of an Angel

*The Night the
Angels Sang*

The First Grandchild

Our first grandchild is the herald
of a new phase in our lives,
and every grandchild that comes
after will reaffirm the wonder of it.

❧ RUTH GOODE ❧

Father, may we our
children lead in paths of
peace to Thy sweet fold.

May ne'er our sin or sad
neglect e'er make them
hard, perverse or cold.

$\mathcal{L}$ove is the doorway
through which the
human soul passes from
selfishness to service and
from solitude to kinship
with all mankind.

⤜ ANONYMOUS ⤛

Home

Home is where affections bind
Gentle hearts in union,
Where voices all are kind,
Together holding sweet
communion.

When grace
is joined with
wrinkles, it is adorable.
There is an unspeakable
dawn in a happy
old age.

❧ VICTOR HUGO ❧

There is never much

trouble in any family

where the children hope

someday to resemble

their parents.

&WILLIAM LYON PHELPS&

Mother Love

The mother love is like God's love; He loves us not because we are lovable, but because it is His nature to love, and because we are His children.

ᕫ EARL RINEY ᕬ

Grandma's Prayer

I pray that, risen from the dead,
I may in glory stand—
A crown, perhaps, upon my head,
But a needle in my hand.
I've never learned to sing or play,
So let no harp be mine;

From birth unto my dying day,
Plain sewing's been my line.
Therefore, accustomed to mend
To plying useful stitches,
I'll be content if asked to mend
The little angel's breeches.

⚘ EUGENE FIELD ⚘

When Grandmama Was Young

Once upon a time
When Grandmama was young,
Foxes played on bagpipes,
Raccoons beat on drums,
Mice danced minuets,
Squirrels two-stepped gaily,
And the unmarried cottontails
Gave tea parties daily.

⊱ ELIZABETH COATSWORTH ⊰

Govern a small family as
you would cook a small
fish, very gently.

⊗ CHINESE PROVERB ⊗

Spare the rod and spoil the
child—that is true. But, beside
the rod, keep an apple to give
him when he has done well.

⊗ MARTIN LUTHER ⊗

If becoming a grandmother was only a matter of choice I should advise every one of you straightaway to become one. There is no fun for old people like it!

⚘ HANNAH WHITALL SMITH ⚘

The happiness of life is made up of minute fractions...a kiss or smile, a kind look, a heartfelt compliment.

SAMUEL TAYLOR COLERIDGE

I can never close my lips where I have opened my heart.

CHARLES DICKENS

Living is learning the meaning of words. That does not mean the long ten syllable words we have to look up in the dictionary. The really great words to master are short ones—work, love, hope, joy, pain, home, child, life, death.

ஐ HALFORD E. LUCCOCK ஐ

You will find, as you look back

upon your life, that the moments when

you have really lived

are the moments when you have

done things in the spirit of love.

Henry Drummond

Praise Her

"Many women do noble things,
but you surpass them all."
Charm is deceptive, and beauty
is fleeting; but a woman who
fears the LORD is to be praised.
Give her the reward she has
earned and let her works bring
her praise at the city gate.

⊱ PROVERBS 31:29–31 ⊰

No soul is desolate as long as there is a human being for whom it can feel trust and reverence.

≈ GEORGE ELIOT ≈

Out of the mouths of babes come words we shouldn't have said in the first place.

Over the river and through the woods,
To grandmother's house we go;
The horse knows the way
To carry the sleigh,
Through the white and drifted snow.

‹ LYDIA MARIA CHILD ›

Parents have lots of trouble solving their children's problems, and children have even more trouble solving their parents' problems.

Good mothers
are married over again at
their daughters' weddings: and
as for subsequent events, who does not
know how ultramaternal grandmothers
are? — in fact a woman, until she is a
grandmother, does not often really
know what to be a mother is.

⁊ WILLIAM MAKEPEACE
THACKERAY⁊

Children and Other Creatures

Children
(like other creatures)
Love the sun,
Like to lie down
In the grass
And roll
(like cats)
Quite free,

Love to sing
(like birds)
And
(like ants)
Love a sugary thing.
And
(like children)
Love to bring
Gifts to grandparents.

෨ FELICE HOLMAN ෨

Our home joys are the most
delightful earth affords, and the
joy of parents in their children
is the most holy joy of humanity.
It makes their hearts pure
and good; it lifts men up to
their Father in heaven.

JOHANN HEINRICH PESTALOZZI

There is no cosmetic for
beauty like happiness.

MARGUERITE, COUNTESS OF BLESSINGTON

We never know the love
of the parent till we
become parents ourselves.

HENRY WARD BEECHER

By the time the youngest

children have learned to

keep the house tidy,

the oldest grandchildren are

on hand to tear it to pieces.

⊱ CHRISTOPHER MORLEY ⊰

Have courage for the sorrows
of life and patience for the
small ones; and when you
have laboriously accomplished
you daily task, go to sleep in
peace. God is awake.

⁂ VICTOR HUGO ⁂

She Was Always There

First grandchildren are
important, and I was the
lucky one in our family
to be my grandmother's
first grandchild. My
grandparents lived nearby
which was fortunate.

Whenever childhood crises occurred—it was easy to flee to the next neighborhood, find Grandmother and pour out one's troubles over milk and cookies at the kitchen table. She was always there.

꙳ MARY MUNGER LUKE ꙳

Praise will transform

the humblest dwelling

to a hallowed heaven.

⊱ FRANCES J. ROBERTS ⊰

Forget Not to Remember

Remember the wonderful blessings
that come to you each day from the
hands of a generous and gracious
God, and forget the irritations that
would detract from your happiness.

Remember the gift of life;
forget your aches and pains.

Remember the privilege of prayer;
forget the negatives that needle you.

Remember the majesty of the mountains; forget the valley of despair. Remember the friends who encourage; forget the frustrations that discourage. Remember to forget your losses, setbacks, and defeats. Don't forget to remember your blessings, your triumphs, and your victories.

WILLIAM ARTHUR WARD

Better to do a good deed
near at home than go
far away to burn incense.

≌ CHINESE PROVERB ≊

A part of kindness
consists in loving people
more than they deserve.

≌ JOSEPH JOUBERT ≊

The Cycle of Life

It is as grandmothers that our mothers come into the fullness of their grace. When a man's mother holds his child in her gladdened arms he is aware of the roundness of life's cycle; of the mystic harmony of life's ways.

ᘏ CHRISTOPHER MORLEY ᘓ

What we desire
our children to become,
we must endeavor
to be before them.

∞ ANDREW COMBE ∞

Generations of Faith

I have been reminded of your sincere faith, which first lived in your grandmother Lois and in your mother Eunice and, I am persuaded, now lives in you also.

᠗ 2 TIMOTHY 1:5 ᠗

A happy family is but
an earlier heaven.

⊰ SIR JOHN BOWRING ⊱

*L*ove understands love;
it needs no talk.

⊰ FRANCES RIDLEY HAVERGAL ⊱

Memories

Oh better than
the minting of a
gold-crowned king
Is the safe-kept
memory of a
lovely thing.

❧ SARA TEASDALE ☙

A Child's Fancy

O little flowers, you love me so,
you could not do without me;
O little birds that come and go,
you sing sweet songs about me;
O little moss, observed by few,
that round the tree is creeping,
you like my head to rest on you, when I
am idly sleeping. And I will make a
promise, dears, that will content you,
maybe; I'll love you through the happy
years, till I'm a nice old lady!

"A"

If things go well with the family,
life is worth living; when the
family falters, life falls apart.

≈ MICHAEL NOVAK ≈

Our great thoughts,
our great affections,
the truths of our life,
never leave us.

≈ WILLIAM MAKEPEACE THACKERAY ≈

If Apples Were Pears

If apples were pears,
And peaches were plums,
And the rose had a different name,
If tigers were bears,
And fingers were thumbs,
I'd love you just the same!

How sweet the words
of truth breathed
from the lips of love.

⃠ J. BEATTIE ⃠

The glow of one warm
thought is to me worth
more than money.

⃠ THOMAS JEFFERSON ⃠

The closest friends I have made all through life have been people who also grew up close to a loved and loving grandmother or grandfather.

ᔥ MARGARET MEAD ᔥ

We only
see a little of the ocean, a few
miles distance from the rocky shore;
but oh! out there beyond—beyond the
eye's horizon there's more—there's more.
We only see a little of God's loving, a
few rich treasures from his mighty store;
But oh! out there beyond—beyond
our life's horizon there's
more—there's more.

Go, labor on; spend and be spent—

Thy joy to do the Father's will; it

is the way the  Master went;

should not the servant tread it still?

HORATIUS BONAR

The proper time to influence the character of a child is about a hundred years before he is born.

﷯ DEAN INGE ﷯

No one is useless in this world who lightens the burden of it for anyone else.

﷯ CHARLES DICKENS ﷯

Cheerfulness and
contentment are
great beautifiers,
and are famous
preservers of
good looks.

∾ CHARLES DICKENS ∾

My

grandmothers were
strong. They followed plows
and bent to toil. They moved
through fields sowing seed. They
touched earth and grain grew.

∞ MARGARET ABIGAIL WALKER ∞

Now that
I've reached the age,
or maybe the stage, where I need
my children morethan they need me,
I really understand how grand it is to
be a grandmother.

~ MARGARET WHITLAM ~

Some people, no matter how old they get, never lose their beauty—they merely move it from their faces into their hearts.

The Grandmother Experience

For me and for every woman I know, no matter how many of our friends have arrived there before us, no matter what we have expected or been told to expect, becoming a grandmother has been a totally new and wonderful but also somewhat strange experience for which nothing seems to have prepared us in advance. And as the children grow and change, we are constantly discovering new aspects of our role in their lives and their effect on ours, even—to our surprise—new aspects of ourselves.

⁎ RUTH GOODE ⁎

Small

wonder we love our

grandchildren. They

are our immortality.

♪ Phyllis McGinley ♪

Whoever lives true life,

will love true love.

❧ Elizabeth Barrett Browning ❧

Love this world through me, Lord.
This world of broken men,
Thou didst love through death, Lord.
Oh, love in me again!
Souls are in despair, Lord.
Oh, make me know and care;
When my life they see,
May they behold Thee,
Oh, love the world through me.

❧ WILL HOUGHTON ❦

$\mathcal{I}$ expect to pass through this world but once; any good thing, therefore, that I can do, or any kindness that I can show to my fellow creatures, let me do it now; let me not defer or neglect it, for I shall not pass this way again.

⊱ MARCUS AURELIUS ANTONINUS ⊰

Little self-denials, little
honesties, little passing words of
sympathy, little nameless acts of
kindness, little silent victories
over favorite temptations—
these are the silent threads of
gold which, when woven together,
gleam out so brightly in the pattern
of life that God approves.

ॐ FREDERIC WILLIAM FARRAR ∞

A sweater is a knitted
garment worn by a child when
his mother feels cold.

ॐ ANONYMOUS ॐ

A family is a unit composed
not only of children, but of men,
women, an occasional animal,
and the common cold.

ॐ OGDEN NASH ॐ

In youth we learn.

In age we understand.

Mother's Lament

(Who Is Stuck at Home While Grandma Is
Out Having the Time of Her Life)

Where have all
the Grandmas gone?
A lobbying in
Washington, back to work
and back to school,
to Peace Corps posts
in Istanbul,

to regional meetings on
woman's rights, to seminars to
raise their sights,
to the tennis courts and
to the races, to Thebes and
Antibes and faraway places,
to castles in Spain and
to Congress—oh dear,
why couldn't she wait for us!

≫ BARBARA SHOOK HAZEN ≪

Where we
love is home, home
that our feet may leave,
but not our hearts.

⊱ OLIVER WENDELL HOLMES ⊰

Human love, though true
and sweet, has been sent
by love more tender, more
complete, more divine.

❧ ADELAIDE A. PROCTER ❧

Young people set their watches,
for right time or wrong,
by the watches of their elders.

❧ ANONYMOUS ❧

The way to love someone is
to lightly run your finger over
that person's soul until you find
a crack, and then gently pour
your love into that crack.

◈ KEITH MILLER ◈

The days may come,

the days may go,

But still the hands

of memories weave

The blissful dreams

of long ago.

∞ GEORGE COOPER ∾

Certain
thoughts are prayers.
There are moments when,
whatever be the attitude
of the body, the soul
is on its knees.

❧ VICTOR HUGO ❧